Full Count

A Baseball Number Book

Written by Brad Herzog and Illustrated by Bruce Langton

Sleeping Bear Press™
310 North Main Street, Suite 300
Chelsea, MI 48118
www.sleepingbearpress.com

© 2009 Sleeping Bear Press is an imprint of Gale, a part of Cengage Learning.

Printed and bound in the United States.

First Edition

10 9 8 7 6 5 4 3 2 1

Library of Congress Cataloging-in-Publication Data

Herzog, Brad.
Full count : a baseball number book / Written by Brad Herzog;
Illustrated by Bruce Langton.
p. cm.
ISBN 978-1-58536-429-9
1. Baseball—Miscellanea—Juvenile literature. 2. Counting—Juvenile
literature. I. Langton, Bruce. II. Title.
GV867.5.H456 2009
796.357—dc22
2009005440

For Jeff Winicour and his remarkable son, Rhythm,
two of the world's most dedicated Cubs fans.
Keep hope alive. Anything is possible.

BRAD

To Brett and Rory–
Thanks for all the great times growing up together
through baseball and your other favorite sports.
What more could a father ask for? You are the best.

BRUCE

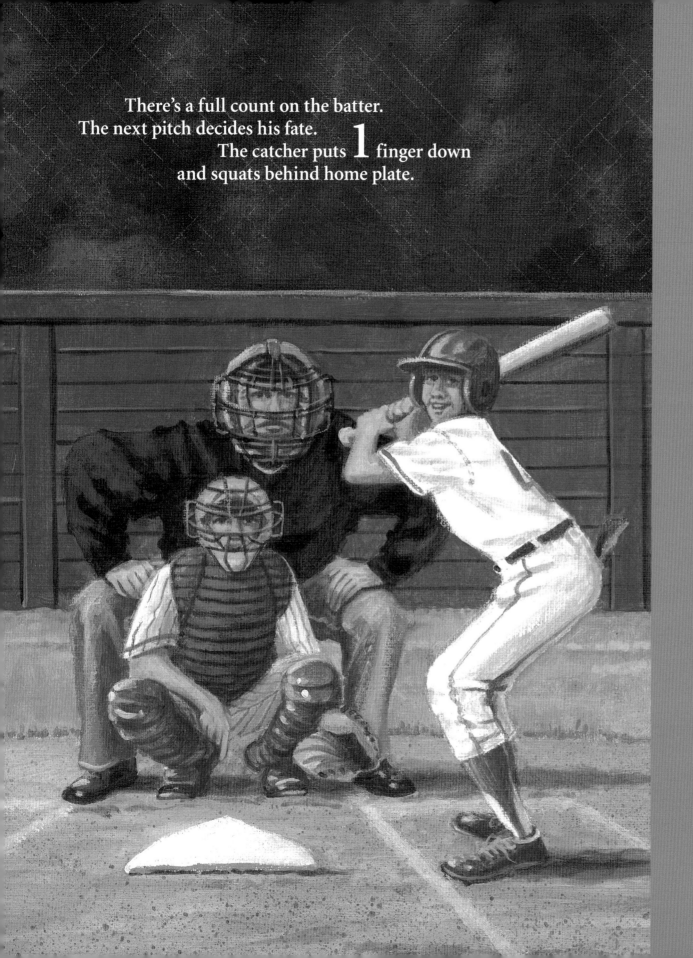

There's a full count on the batter.
The next pitch decides his fate.
The catcher puts 1 finger down
and squats behind home plate.

No matter what the count is on the batter (a full count means three balls and two strikes), the pitcher and catcher must agree on what pitch is coming next. That way, the catcher knows what to expect. He holds his glove just below his left knee (so the opposing team's third-base coach can't see the sign). Then, with his throwing hand, he shows one finger (which usually means the pitcher should throw a fastball), two fingers (a curveball), or three fingers (another off-speed pitch). Each of these signs may be flashed in different sequences. The pitcher knows which one is the correct sign. For example, with a man on second base, the third sign shown might be the real one.

Communication between the pitcher and catcher is also important for safety reasons. Once, in the early 1990s, Seattle Mariners catcher Matt Sinatro forgot which sign he gave to pitcher Randy Johnson. Sinatro expected a slider, but Johnson threw a blazing fastball...which hit the umpire in the stomach!

one
1

2 If one baseball game is great fun,
aren't 2 games even better?
This occasion has its own name.
    It's called a doubleheader.

Ernie Banks, a Hall of Fame shortstop who played for the Chicago Cubs, used to say, "It's a beautiful day for a ballgame—let's play two!" Back when Banks played (in the 1950s, 1960s, and 1970s) doubleheaders—two games played on the same day—were a regular feature of the major league schedule. In baseball's early days, there were even three instances of *tripleheaders*! But nowadays, while doubleheaders are still common in college baseball, they only happen in the major leagues if teams have to make up a game that was postponed due to bad weather.

One of the more unique doubleheaders occurred on July 8, 2000, when the New York Yankees took on their crosstown rivals, the New York Mets. The first game was played at Shea Stadium, home of the Mets. The Yankees won 4-2. Then both teams rode buses to Yankee Stadium (while many fans took the subway) and played the second game of the double-header. The Yankees again won 4-2.

two

2

Everybody knows that it's "one, two, three strikes you're out at the old ball game." And every pitcher hopes to strike out three batters in a row, which is known as a 1-2-3 inning. But occasionally there are actually four outs in an inning—sometimes even four strikeouts! This feat has occurred nearly 50 times in major league history. It happens when the catcher is unable to cleanly catch a third strike. In that case, the batter may try to reach first base before being tagged or thrown out. The pitcher is credited with a strikeout—perhaps even the third strikeout of the inning. But if the batter reaches base, then it isn't actually the third out.

In Game 4 of the 1941 World Series, Brooklyn Dodgers catcher Mickey Owen failed to catch a third strike that would have ended the game against the New York Yankees. The runner reached first base, and the Yankees rallied to win the game and the championship.

three

It's **3** strikes and you're out,
and three outs complete the inning.
Three straight victories is called a sweep.
The team just keeps on winning.

When the All-American Girls Baseball League began,
only **4** teams played the game.
But now those women who took the field
have a place in the Hall of Fame.

In the early 1940s, during World War II, many of the nation's top players traded their baseball uniforms for soldiers' uniforms. With many of the game's stars gone, Chicago Cubs owner Philip K. Wrigley feared that attendance would drop. So he decided to organize another league to attract fans—a league for women. From 1943 through 1954, more than 600 women competed in the All-American Girls Professional Baseball League. Some of the players were as young as 15 years old.

The league started with just four teams, each located in a small city in the Midwest, but it grew to include as many as ten teams. They had names like the Kenosha Comets, the Rockford Peaches, and the South Bend Blue Sox.

Although the rules evolved over the years (it began as a softball league), and although the women were forced to play in skirts, some very good baseball was on display. Occasionally, the women's teams drew even more fans than their major league counterparts. The National Baseball Hall of Fame (in Cooperstown, New York) now has a permanent exhibit celebrating the accomplishments of women in baseball.

four

4

The game of tee ball is a sport in which young players (usually ages four to eight years old) can have fun while developing baseball and softball skills like hitting, running, fielding, and throwing. A baseball is placed on an adjustable batting tee atop home plate, and two teams take turns hitting the ball. Maximum participation is the goal. In most tee ball leagues, all players on the defensive team can play in the field every inning (there is usually no pitcher), and all players on the hitting team are allowed to bat once per inning. Keeping score isn't common. Having fun is.

It is estimated that more than two million kids play the game around the world, and more than one-third of them are girls. Some lucky tee ball teams have even been invited to Washington, D.C., to play a special game on the South Lawn of the White House!

five

5

At the age of **5** years old,
boys and girls can play a game
of baseball without pitchers.
And tee ball is its name.

When keeping score in baseball,
the shortstop is number 6.
Starting a 6-4-3 double play
is one of his coolest tricks.

Both a baseball game's official scorer and many fans in the stands use a scorecard to record the result of every at-bat in the game. Many fans have their own way of keeping score, but some methods are used by nearly everybody.

For instance, a numbering system is used to describe playing positions: pitcher (1), catcher (2), first baseman (3), second baseman (4), third baseman (5), shortstop (6), left fielder (7), center fielder (8), and right fielder (9). When an out is made, scorekeepers record the combination of defensive players making the play. So a fly ball that is caught by the center fielder would be recorded as **8**. If a third baseman fields a ground ball and throws to the first baseman, it is marked as **5-3**. If a ball is hit to the shortstop, who tosses it to the second baseman, who steps on second base to force a runner and then throws to the first baseman to complete a double play...that's a **6-4-3 DP**.

six

6

There may be no more dramatic event in baseball than the seventh game of the World Series. In the best-of-seven series, it is winner-take-all excitement!

Perhaps the most memorable Game 7 occurred in the 1960 World Series when the Pittsburgh Pirates faced off against the New York Yankees at Pittsburgh's Forbes Field. With the game tied 9-9 in the bottom of the ninth inning, Pirates second base-man Bill Mazeroski came to bat. Although he is in the Hall of Fame, "Maz" was elected mostly for his amazing defensive skills. He wasn't an outstanding hitter. But this time he rose to the occasion, hitting a home run over the left field wall and giving the joyous home fans their first baseball champion-ship in 35 years.

The moment is so treasured in Pittsburgh that a group of people celebrate its anni-versary every October 13. They gather at the old location of Forbes Field and listen to the entire radio broadcast of the game. The Pirates always win!

seven

7

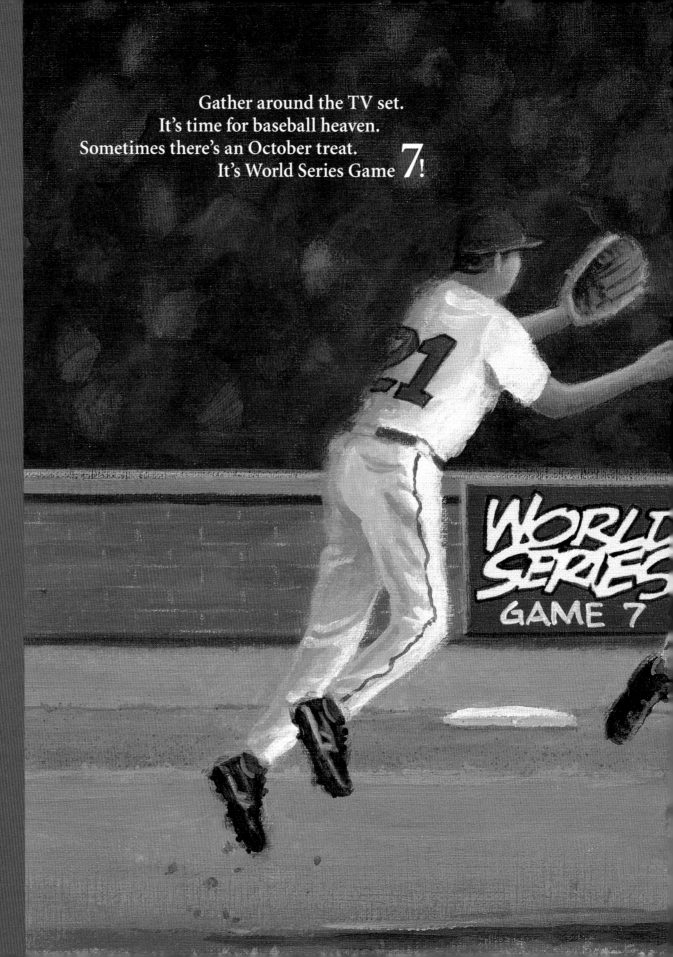

Gather around the TV set.
It's time for baseball heaven.
Sometimes there's an October treat.
It's World Series Game 7!

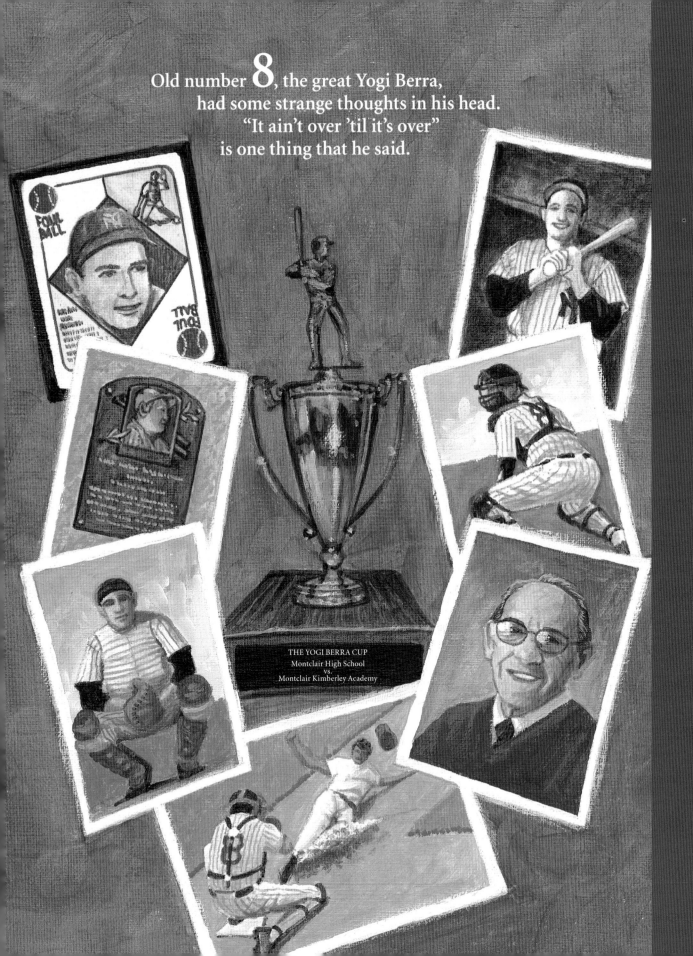

Old number **8**, the great Yogi Berra,
had some strange thoughts in his head.
"It ain't over 'til it's over"
is one thing that he said.

THE YOGI BERRA CUP
Montclair High School
vs.
Montclair Kimberley Academy

During his 19-year-career with the New York Yankees, Yogi Berra (who wore uniform #8) was a 15-time All-Star, a 10-time World Series champion, and a three-time American League Most Valuable Player. But the Hall of Fame catcher may be best known for his unintentionally funny comments. The following are some of Berra's most famous sayings:

"You can see a lot just by observing."

"A home opener is always exciting, no matter if it's home or on the road."

"Why buy good luggage? You only use it when you travel."

"Nobody goes there anymore. It's too crowded."

"A nickel ain't worth a dime anymore."

"Baseball is ninety percent mental. The other half is physical."

"I usually take a two-hour nap from one o'clock to four."

"It gets late early out there."

"I didn't really say everything I said."

eight
8

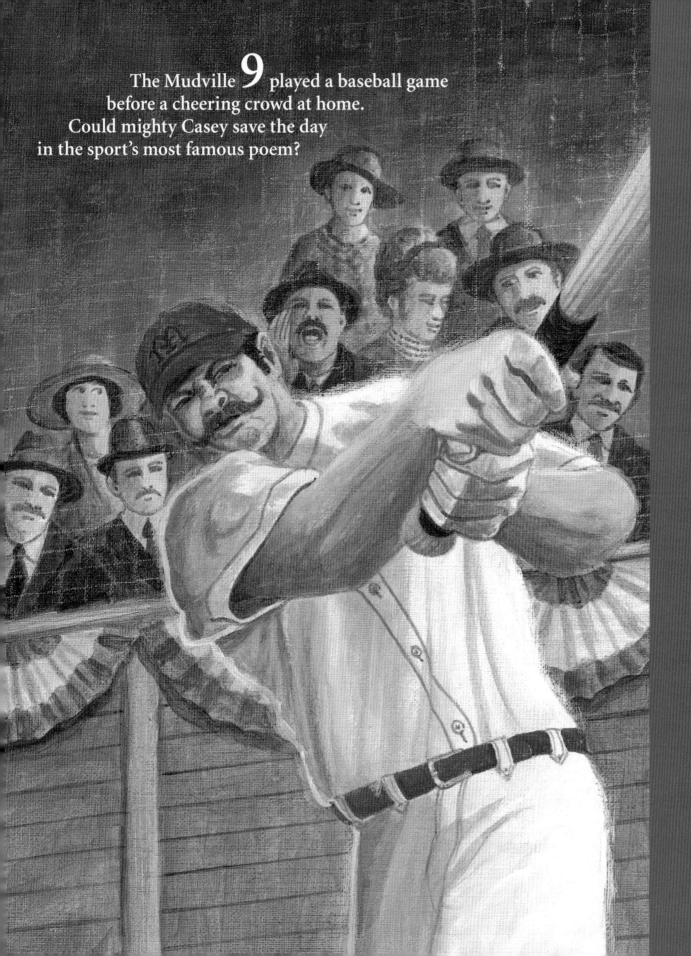

The Mudville **9** played a baseball game before a cheering crowd at home. Could mighty Casey save the day in the sport's most famous poem?

*The outlook wasn't brilliant
for the Mudville Nine that day;
The score stood four to two with
but one inning more to play...*

Those are the first two lines of "Casey at the Bat," a poem written by Ernest L. Thayer in June 1888. It became an instant hit when actor DeWolf Hopper recited it in front of an audience a couple of months later. Hopper would repeat his performance nearly ten thousand times over the next decade, turning the poem into a classic piece of sports literature. "Casey at the Bat" continues until there are two outs and two men on base in the bottom of that final inning. Then the home team's star, mighty Casey himself, steps up to the plate. As the crowd cheers, he takes strike one, then strike two... Finally, the poem comes to a stirring end:

*Oh, somewhere in this favored land
the sun is shining bright;
The band is playing somewhere,
and somewhere hearts are light,
And somewhere men are laughing,
and somewhere children shout;
But there is no joy in Mudville—
mighty Casey has struck out.*

nine
9

In the mid-nineteenth century, the most popular team sport in America made use of a bat and ball. However, it wasn't baseball. It was a somewhat similar game called cricket. But that would soon change. In the late 1860s, Harry Wright, a star cricket player who was born in England, was hired to manage a new baseball team called the Cincinnati Red Stockings. He hired the best players money could buy on what was the first openly all-professional baseball club (before then, many top players had been secretly paid). The team's total payroll was $9,300.

The Red Stockings toured the country, traveling nearly 12 thousand miles by train and popularizing the game immensely. The 10 players on the team became famous, mostly because they wouldn't lose. They won every one of their 57 games in 1869 and ran their winning streak to 81 games the following year before the team was disbanded. By then, baseball was on its way to becoming the national pastime.

ten

10

The Cincinnati Red Stockings
were baseball's first group of pros.
A team of just **10** players,
they beat most all their foes.

When Joe Nuxhall signed a contract with the Cincinnati Reds in 1944, he was so young that he had to get special permission from his high school principal! On June 10 of that year, he was sent in to pitch the ninth inning of a major league game, making him the youngest player of the twentieth century—at the age of 15 years, 10 months, and 11 days.

The tall left-hander didn't do very well. He retired two of the first three batters he faced, but he wound up allowing five walks, two hits, one wild pitch, and five runs before his manager removed him from the game. Nuxhall had to pitch for seven years in the minor leagues before he received a second chance in the Big Show. This time, he was ready. He spent—you guessed it!—15 more years in the major leagues, collecting 135 wins, and even pitching in an All-Star Game. Nuxhall later became a longtime Reds announcer.

fifteen

15

At age 15 most baseball players are competing in high school ball. But the youngest player in the major leagues was **15**-year-old Joe Nuxhall.

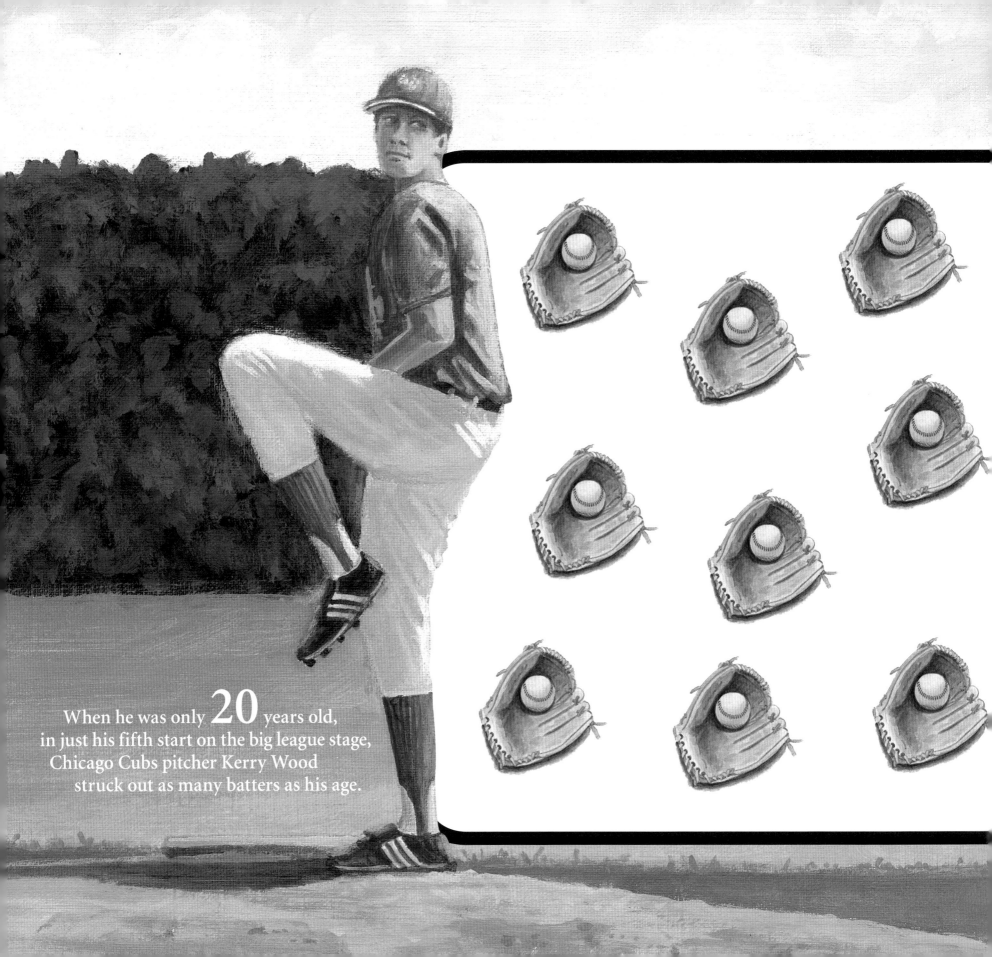

When he was only **20** years old,
in just his fifth start on the big league stage,
Chicago Cubs pitcher Kerry Wood
struck out as many batters as his age.

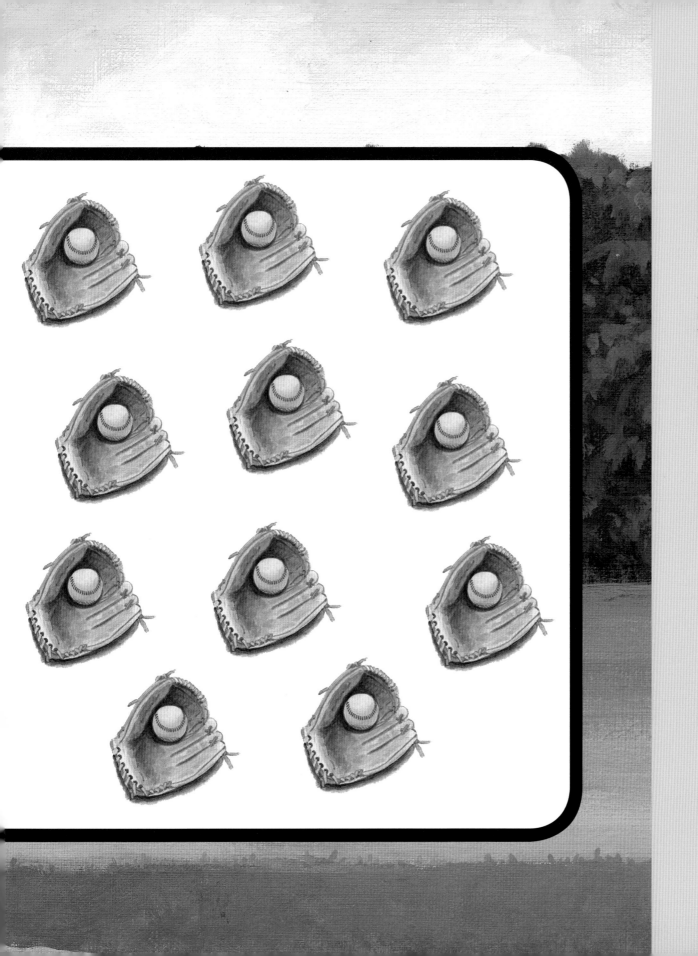

In all of major league baseball history, only three pitchers have struck out 20 batters in the first nine innings of a game. Roger Clemens did it twice—in 1986 and 1996 with the Boston Red Sox. Randy Johnson did it last—in 2001 with the Arizona Diamondbacks. In between, on May 6, 1998, 20-year-old Chicago Cubs pitcher Kerry Wood became only the second man ever to strike out as many batters as his age. The first to do it was Cleveland Indians star Bob Feller. In 1936, Feller struck out 17 batters at the age of 17!

However, 20 strikeouts are not actually the most in a complete major league game. On September 12, 1962, Tom Cheney of the Washington Senators pitched a complete 16-inning game against the Baltimore Orioles and struck out 21 batters! Because Cheney only won 19 games in his entire career, he has been largely forgotten. But his record still stands.

twenty
20

Only players on a team's 25-man roster may suit up for a major league baseball game. But another important member of the team is the batboy, who is now required to be age 14 or older.

A batboy works hard on the day of a home game. Often, he arrives at the ballpark several hours before the game starts. He may haul out the catcher's gear and towels and bats, bring sunflower seeds and bubble-gum to the dugout area, and even do errands for some of the players. During the game, his jobs might include retrieving discarded bats and handing new baseballs to the umpire.

In return the batboy receives many perks. He is allowed to pose for the team photo and stand with the players during the national anthem. He gets paid for his job (including end-of-season tips from the players). He wears a major league uniform (although it is usually nameless and num-berless). And, if the team is good enough, he can even earn a championship ring!

twenty-five

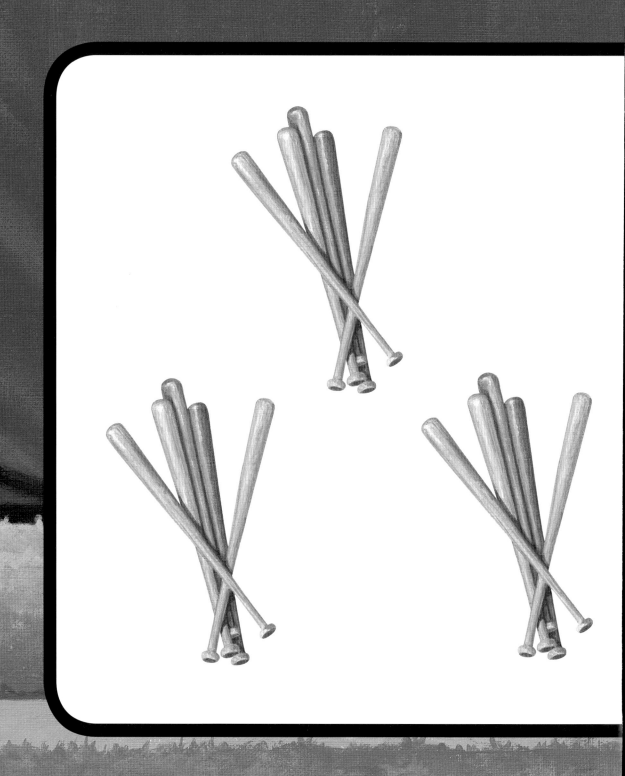

There are **25** men on each major league team.
That's how many are allowed.
But the batboy wears a uniform, too.
You can spot him from the crowd.

PLAYING YEARS
1947 - 1956

JACKIE ROBINSON

50 years after Jackie Robinson
showed what he could do,
all of baseball honored him
by retiring number 42.

On April 15, 1947, 28-year-old Jackie Robinson changed sports forever simply by stepping out on the field for the Brooklyn Dodgers. He was the first African-American to play in the major leagues, a truly monumental and long-overdue occasion. Robinson would go on to win many honors, including a Rookie of the Year Award (in 1947), a Most Valuable Player Award (in 1949), and election to the Baseball Hall of Fame (in 1962).

Exactly 50 years after that barrier-breaking day—on April 15, 1997—Major League Baseball honored Robinson by retiring his jersey number. No new players would be allowed to wear number 42. It would belong to Robinson forever. Ten years later, on the 60th anniversary of Robinson's first major league appearance, baseball came up with another way of honoring him. For one day, every player was invited to wear his number. More than 200 players did so. In fact, six teams had everyone in uniform wearing number 42—players, coaches, managers, even batboys!

fifty
50

It has been nearly **75** years
since Little League Baseball® got its start.
It began with just three teams.
Now thousands of kids take part.

Little League Baseball® began in 1939 with a three-team league in Williamsport, Pennsylvania. Today, more than seven thousand teams from around the world participate in the Little League International Tournament. But only 16 of these teams play their way to the Little League Baseball World Series (for 11- and 12-year-olds), which takes place each August in Williamsport. Representing eight regions in the United States and eight international regions, the 16 teams compete in front of as many as 250,000 spectators over ten days. By the end, only two teams remain to play in the championship game at Howard J. Lamade Stadium. The winner is truly a world champion!

There is also a Girls Little League Softball® division, which holds its annual World Series in August. But the girls play on the other side of the country—at Alpenrose Field in Portland, Oregon. Past champions have come from many regions of the country—from Tennessee and Texas to Pennsylvania and Puerto Rico.

seventy-
five

75

Who is the fastest pitcher in baseball history? Many people name Nolan Ryan, who set two records that may never be broken by recording 5,714 career strikeouts and tossing an incredible seven no-hitters. Ryan was listed in the *Guinness Book of World Records* when he threw a 100.9-mile-per-hour fastball during a game in 1974. But since then, several dozen players have broken the magic 100-mile-per-hour mark on the radar gun (which measures pitch speed), and some have even exceeded Ryan's speed.

Although the discussion of fastest fastballs often mentions many all-time greats—from Hall of Famer Walter Johnson to future Hall of Famer Randy Johnson—some former players insist that an obscure player named Steve Dalkowski was the fastest of all. He stood just under six feet tall, wore thick glasses, and struck out 1,396 batters in 995 minor league innings. But he never made it to the major leagues because he also walked 1,354 batters! The lesson: It's great to throw fast, but you also have to throw strikes.

one
hundred
100

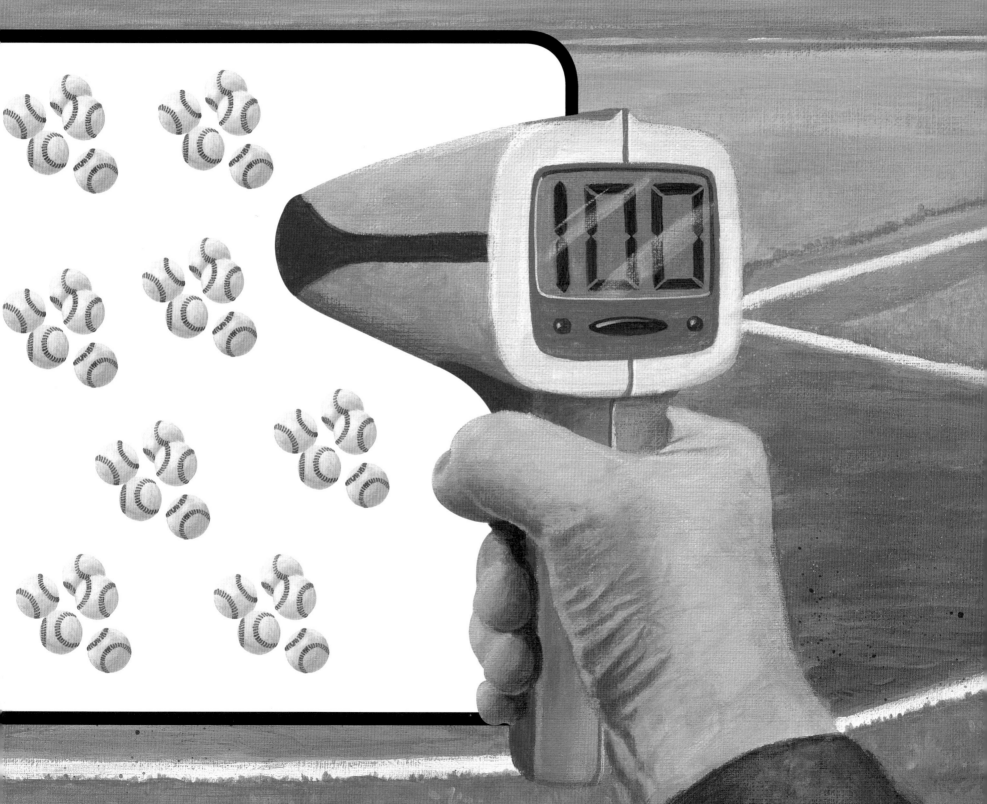

The fastest hurlers in baseball
throw with so much power
reach **100** that some of their speediest pitches
miles per hour.

Brad Herzog

Brad Herzog lives on California's Monterey Peninsula with his wife, Amy, and his two sons, Luke and Jesse. As a freelance writer, he has won several awards from the Council for the Advancement and Support of Education, including a Grand Gold Medal for best magazine article of the year. Brad has published more than two dozen books, including two memoirs about his travels through small-town America. His alphabet books for Sleeping Bear Press include *A is for Amazing Moments: A Sports Alphabet* and *S is for Save the Planet: A How-to-Be Green Alphabet*. Visit his Web site at www.bradherzog.com.

Bruce Langton

Bruce Langton's unmistakable style and unique ability to capture true-life scenes have won him numerous national awards for both his nature paintings and children's books. After a successful career in both commercial illustration and wildlife art, Bruce switched priorities to focus on children, finding a career as a nationally renowned children's book illustrator. Bruce resides in Indiana with his wife, Rebecca, and two sons, Brett and Rory, along with their African Grey parrot, a guinea pig named Microsoft, and Wrigley, a black schnauzer.